A-02

# ASIAN
# MARKET ECONOMIES

*ISEAS Current Economic Affairs Series*

# ASIAN MARKET ECONOMIES

## Challenges of a Changing International Environment

Ross Garnaut
*Australian National University*

 ASEAN ECONOMIC RESEARCH UNIT
INSTITUTE OF SOUTHEAST ASIAN STUDIES

Published by
Institute of Southeast Asian Studies
Heng Mui Keng Terrace
Pasir Panjang
Singapore 0511

*The responsibility for facts and opinions expressed in this publication rests exclusively with the author and his interpretations do not necessarily reflect the views or the policy of the Institute or its supporters.*

**Cataloguing in Publication Data**

Garnaut, Ross.
   Asian market economies : challenges of a changing international environment.
   (ISEAS current economic affairs series)
1. Asia—Commercial policy.
2. Asia—Economic conditions—1945-
3. International economic relations.
I. Title.
II. Series.
HF1583 G23        1994        sls93-99790

ISBN 981-3016-78-7
ISSN 0218-2114

Typeset by The Fototype Business
Printed in Singapore by Singapore National Printers.

# CONTENTS

## ACKNOWLEDGEMENTS

An earlier version of this paper was first presented at the international conference "Southeast Asia: Challenges of the 21st Century" organized by the Institute of Southeast Asian Studies, 20 August-1 September 1993, Singapore on the occasion of its 25th anniversary.

The author is grateful to Yiping Huang and Ligang Song for their efficient assistance in assembling data and materials for this work, and to Peter Drysdale for agreeing to use of output from their joint work.

# I THE ASIAN MARKET ECONOMIES

In the early 1980s, the geographic boundaries defined in the title of this paper would have been drawn very differently from today.

Then, as now, there would have been no ambiguity about the inclusion of the ASEAN economies, Japan, Hong Kong, Taiwan and the Republic of Korea. Then, as now, there would have been no ambiguity about the exclusion of the Democratic People's Republic of Korea. But that is the end of the consistency over time.

The People's Republic of China is now best considered as an Asian market economy. It was certainly not a market economy a decade ago. A large majority of production of goods and services is now independent of the state plan, and what is left of the plan scrambles to keep up with the signals emitted by powerful market forces.

When did the switch-over take place in China? There is no need, and no opportunity, to be precise. I would date it somewhere between the Thirteenth Communist Party Congress in 1987 and the Fourteenth in 1992 — between the Chinese Communist Party's acceptance of the doctrine of the "preliminary stage of socialism", and its acceptance that China was a "socialist market economy". If a journalist

1

were pressing me for a single date, and I was too tired to resist, I would say May 1991, when large price adjustments for agricultural products including grain paved the path for market determination of food prices.

Are the economies of Indochina market economies? Vietnam's price and enterprise reforms are much younger than China's, but have proceeded more rapidly. The dynamic rural enterprises that have defined the "market-oriented" character of the Chinese economy since the mid-1980s do not so far have counterparts in Vietnam. The inflationary macro-economic environment is less conducive to smooth operation of markets than in China. But there is no doubt about the direction of change in Vietnam, and it is, as least, an Asian emerging market economy.

South Asia is hardest of all to define. Markets, relative to state power, are now less important in resource allocation in india than in China. The Indian economy is much less oriented towards international markets — although the difference is not so great if we adjust China's GDP for obvious miscalculation in the standard international data. In these past two years, India, too, is changing in the direction of a market economy, carrying with it the pressures and constraints of a huge and rambling democracy. The collapse of the Soviet Union dealt a fatal blow to the failing intellectual support for command planning in India, and reduced India's options as a major market almost disappeared almost overnight. The economic success of China has placed international geostrategic and domestic political pressure on Indian economic policy and performance. It will take longer in India. However, over the past two years India has entered a period of market-oriented reform which will lead to much more intense interaction with the international and Asia-Pacific economies, and substantially more rapid economic growth — if several notches below the strongest performers of East Asia. The most telling sign that India is firmly, if slowly, on the path of market-oriented reform, is the changed tone of debate about economic policy, in intellectual circles, and more broadly in policy-relevant public discussion.

The changed climate of opinion in India is affecting discussion and policy elsewhere in South Asia, including Pakistan.

So where are the boundaries of the Asian market economies? This paper focuses primarily on the East Asian economies that are participating in the Asia-Pacific Economic Co-operation (APEC) forum. And I will keep in mind the economies of Indochina and South Asia, as emerging market economies.

## II  THE INTERNATIONAL ENVIRONMENT

When discussing in international economic environment, the political and strategic environment cannot be ignored, however — if only because it intrudes directly into the forces shaping the international trading rules.

The end of the Cold War is reshaping the international environment of the East Asian market economies, as decisively as the Cold War itself shaped international economic relations in the 1950s and 1960s. The end of the Cold War has brought new opportunities: through the spur it has given to internationally-oriented growth in India and Indochina; and the opportunity it has provided for gradual economic change in North Korea in ways that will eventually facilitate internationally-oriented integration of the two Korean economies. It has also brought opportunities to China, as the greater security on its long land borders allows more confident and complete application of national energies to the tasks of economic reform and development.

But there are also challenges, and threats, to the continuation of internationally-oriented growth in the new environment.

The collapse of the Soviet Union, and the difficulties that its successor states and the states of Eastern Europe are having in establishing institutional bases for market-oriented development, are placing great strain on the whole European economy. In Germany this is compounded by the special problems of reunification. This has deepened and attenuated recession, and turned community opinion defensively inward on all matters related to the international trading system. The problems of Western European adjustment to market-oriented development in the East are formidable, and as yet only faintly appreciated. There will be exacerbation of inter-continental discrimination in European trade, in result if not intent. But even the intent will be increasingly unreliable, as jarring comparisons of East Asian and European economic performance, and a persistent competitive challenge in global including European markets, breeds resentment, at its worst paranoia, and more defensive and inward-looking approaches to trade policy.

There are still, and there will remain, forces in support of open trade in Western Europe. But the whole polity of Western Europe cannot be expected to provide leadership of, or on balance, consistent support for, the open, multi-lateral trading system.

The effects of the end of the Cold War on U.S. support

for the post-war framework of open multilateral trade are at once more complex, more important to economic development in East Asia and the Western Pacific, and potentially more dangerous.

Rapid, internationally-oriented economic growth was established in Japan and Hong Kong in the early 1950s, in Taiwan, Singapore and Korea in the early and mid-1960s, and later in Malaysia, Thailand, mainland China and Indonesia. It was established in the context of the open, multilateral trading system based on the General Agreement on Tariffs and Trade (GATT) that was built in the immediate aftermath of World War II. The system through its strongest years depended heavily on the United States' commitment, leadership, and preparedness to accept adjustment in response to developments in the comparative advantage and export capacity of East Asian economies.

While the post-war trading system, and American support for it, had its origins in the memory of the trade-destroying policies of the 1930s and in post-war idealism, American commitment was sustained by the geostrategic imperatives of the Cold War. The tensions that have arisen in the United States' relations with the international economy in recent years are reminders of this powerful reality.

Richard Snape remarked recently that, for all the imperfections of GATT, it provides the essential legal framework of U.S. trade policy that superseded the Smoot-Hawley tariff of 1931 (Snape 1993). Without GATT, or a viable successor, the law and the political economy of trade policy are subject to powerful pressures in the direction of the protectionism and bilateralism of the 1930s.

Without the United States' perception of an overwhelming strategic interest in the prosperity and stability of Japan,

Korea, Taiwan and the ASEAN states, and in the entrenchment of internationally-oriented growth in China, the political balance is much more open to the old, prosaic domestic pressures on trade policy.

This is the new environment of diminished U.S. commitment to open and multilateral trade. It is the environment of the damaging tensions in Japanese-American trade relations. And it is part of the immensely complex environment of Sino-American economic relations, which is then overlain by divergent perspectives on human rights, and concerns about the implications of Chinese arms sales on the stability of relations amongst states in the new strategic order that is emerging in the aftermath of the Cold War.

It is powerfully in the interests of Western Pacific including East Asian states that a framework of open and multilateral trade is maintained in this new environment. It is an essential interest of the emerging market economies of Asia — India and the South Asian states, Vietnam and Indochina — and also of Russia, and of the large part of the world that would benefit from economic stability and development in the Commonwealth of Independent States (CIS).

With colleagues throughout the Western Pacific, and with some in North America, I have been saying for several years that the new model of trade policy and economic growth that has emerged in the Western Pacific since the mid-1980s provides an opportunity for maintaining open, multilateral trade now that the United States has lost the will to lead. I have argued that APEC, with full North American participation provides the vehicle for binding the two sides of the Pacific into commitment to open trade.

It is necessary to explore the contemporary relevance of this vision of the Asia-Pacific and international trading system. This vision must now contend with an awkward reality, that a substantial part of the intellectual and political constituency for open trade in the United States has formed the view that multilateral free trade is no longer politically viable; that "Congress would not tolerate free riders" on any unilateral or regional trade liberalization on a most-favoured-nation basis.

This is the great immediate challenge to the Asian market economies in the changing international economic environment.

# III RECENT DEVELOPMENTS IN EAST ASIAN ECONOMIES

Since the mid-1980s, more than half of the increase in world production of goods and services has occurred in East Asia. Between 1986 and 1991, growth in Japan added annual output equivalent to an economy the size of France. Internationally-oriented growth became firmly entrenched in East Asia's most populous economies, China and Indonesia, and commenced in Vietnam. Most remarkably, strong growth in the region's developing countries continued undiminished in the early 1990s, despite deep and prolonged recession in the advanced industrial economies of the northern hemisphere. As rapid growth has become established in each of these countries, foreign trade has expanded more rapidly than output and expenditure, although less outstandingly so in Japan than in the region's developing economies.

It happens that the East Asian economies which have grown rapidly through the post-war period have had initial relative resource endowments that are very different from those of the established industrial economies. Japan, Hong Kong, Taiwan, Singapore, Korea and the coastal provinces of mainland China are all densely populated by the standards of the established industrial economies of the North Atlantic, or the rest of the world. Their patterns of specialization in international trade are therefore distinctive, both in the early stages of industrialization when incomes are low, and later when they are high. This increases pressures for structural adjustment in the rest of the world as their foreign trade expands, at the same time as it expands the potential gains from trade. It also leads to criticism that East Asia does not behave "normally" in its trade relations with the rest of the world, and to arguments that the old trade rules are not suitable for the new big players.

The emergence of East Asia as one of three major centres of production and trade, alongside Western Europe and North America has placed great strain on the international trading system. The adjustment strains associated with East Asian growth, coming as they did at a time of slower growth and higher unemployment in the North Atlantic economies, fractured the system in several ways: most importantly, the huge exceptions in the rules on textiles, and the 'grey areas'.

The exception for agriculture had different origins, and once created by the North Atlantic, was accepted readily as an excuse for avoiding adjustment in the newly rich Northeast Asian economies.

Separately, by the 1980s, the post-war rules were recognized as being inadequate, and requiring development for the management of new forms of trade, including in services, and the related matters of intellectual property rights.

Hence the Uruguay Round. It was supported by the

United States and Japan (and some in Europe) to extend the rules to new areas. It was supported in the Americas, Australasia and Southeast Asia to bring in one old exception (agriculture) and to commit developing countries more tightly to the rules. The Uruguay Round was supported (and on some issues led) by Western Pacific, including developing, economies to constrain the exceptions related to manufactured goods and (for Southeast Asia and Australasia) also to remove the exception for agriculture.

There is an important sense in which the weight and adjustment strain of East Asia's internationally oriented growth, and East Asia's comparative success through the 1980s and early 1990s, increased tendencies to discriminatory regionalism in Europe and North America. It was this factor in the acceleration of moves towards Western European economic integration, and, alongside frustration with slow progress in the Uruguay Round, towards the formation of the North American Free Trade Area (NAFTA).

By the early 1990s, these and other moves towards discriminatory regionalism constituted threats to the liberal multilateral trading system as important as those that the Uruguay Round had been established to remove.

## IV   THE GROWING WEIGHT OF EAST ASIA

As the weight of East Asia and the Pacific in world affairs continues to increase, the commitment to the old verities of liberal trade in this region could be crucial in holding back the new tides in the old, North Atlantic industrial countries.

Continued growth in East Asia is likely to be the primary

influence on world trade and economic growth in the next quarter century and beyond, just as it has been in the last. The emergence of East Asia has had a dramatic effect on the structure of world output, and even more so on the structure of world trade. Charts 1 and 2 illustrate these huge shifts in the structure of world production, trade and global economic power.

East Asia accounted for just over 17 per cent of world production in 1980; at the end of the century it can be expected to be over 28 per cent. Already the region accounts for a fifth of world trade, a larger share than North America, and by the year 2000, East Asia's share is expected to be closer to one-third of world trade. These ratios will not stop changing at the millennium. One consequence is that, in the future, the rest of the world will find itself reacting to the forces of economic policy-making in East Asia, as it has done to those of the United States for the past half century.

In East Asia in recent years, structural change and growth have been mutually reinforcing; providing new markets, and an increasingly sophisticated and dynamic regional economy.

There has been extensive unilateral market opening and deregulation in most Western Pacific economies. Their re-markable growth performance has confirmed the prediction of economic theory that the greatest benefit from unilateral trade liberalization accrues to those who undertake it. The benefits have been multiplied by the fact that many neighbouring economies have taken similar unilateral market-opening decisions. The process of progressive trade liberalization amongst Northeast and Southeast Asian economies, has been described elsewhere as a game of "prisoners delight" (Garnaut 1991; Drysdale and Garnaut 1993) built around

Chart 1(a)
Share of World Output, 1980

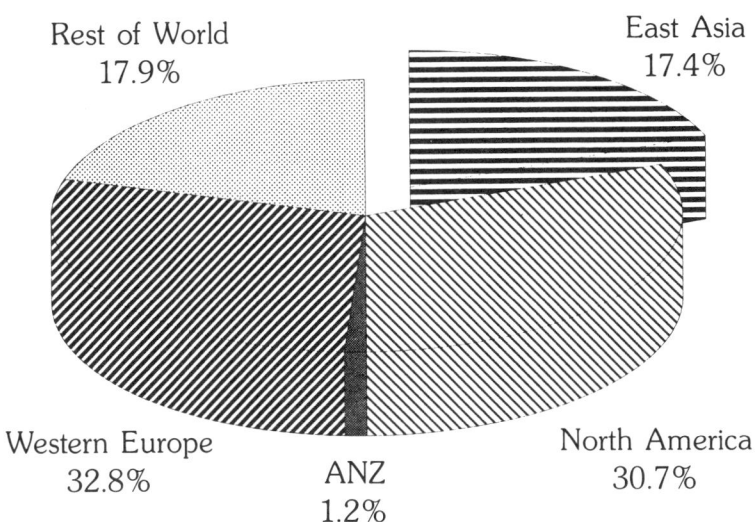

Rest of World
17.9%

East Asia
17.4%

Western Europe
32.8%

ANZ
1.2%

North America
30.7%

SOURCE: Projections by Australia-Japan Research Centre using data from International Economic Databank, Australian National University, Canberra, July 1992. Note that the China output numbers are 2.5 times those conventionally applied in the past by the World Bank (1992), representing a conservative application of insights from recent research (Garnaut and Ma 1993).

## Chart 1(b)
## Share of World Output, 1990

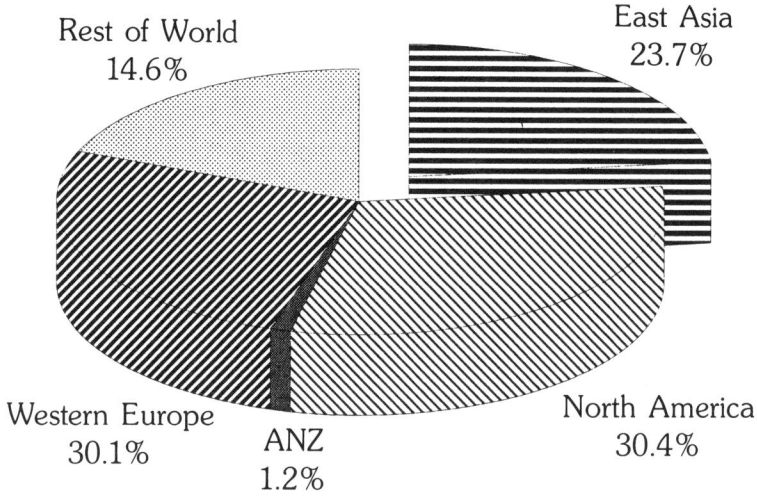

Rest of World 14.6%

East Asia 23.7%

Western Europe 30.1%

ANZ 1.2%

North America 30.4%

SOURCE: Projections by Australia-Japan Research Centre using data from International Economic Databank, Australian National University, Canberra, July 1992. Note that the China output numbers are 2.5 times those conventionally applied in the past by the World Bank (1992), representing a conservative application of insights from recent research (Garnaut and Ma 1993).

## Chart 1(c)
## Share of World Output, 2000

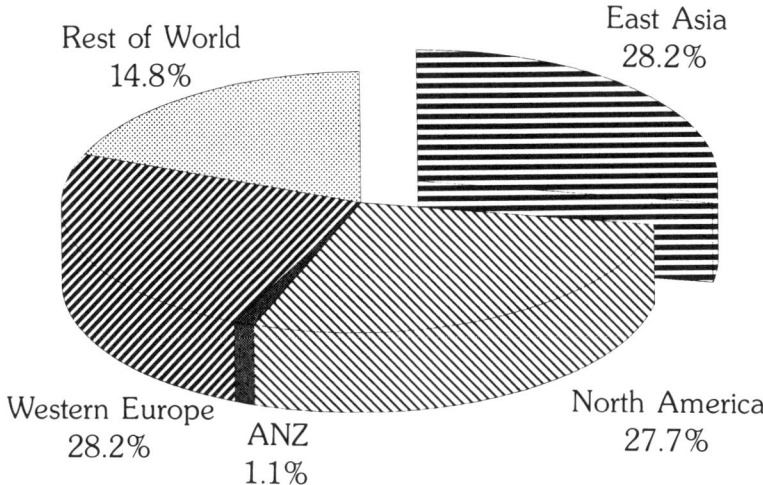

SOURCE: Projections by Australia-Japan Research Centre using data from International Economic Databank, Australian National University, Canberra, July 1992. Note that the China output numbers are 2.5 times those conventionally applied in the past by the World Bank (1992), representing a conservative application of insights from recent research (Garnaut and Ma 1993).

Chart 2(a)
Share of Trade, 1980

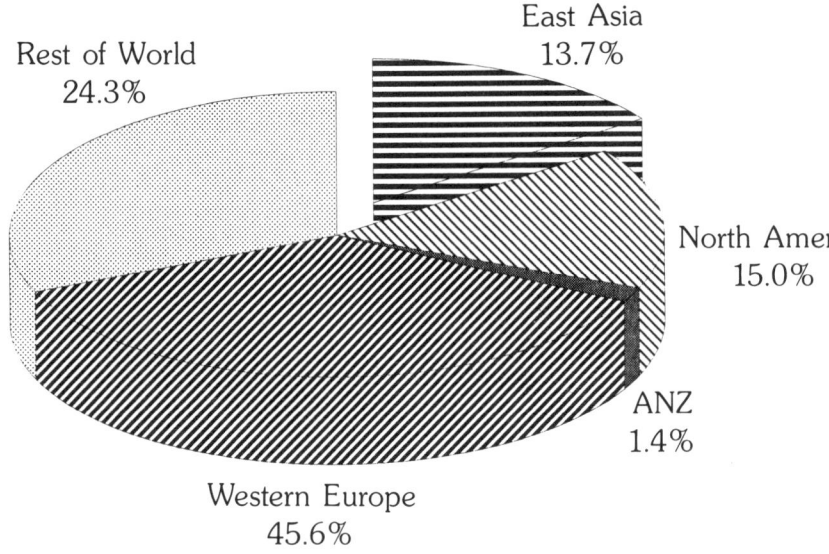

East Asia
13.7%

Rest of World
24.3%

North Ameri
15.0%

ANZ
1.4%

Western Europe
45.6%

SOURCE: Projections by Australia-Japan Research Centre using para-
meters of output growth and trade intensities calculated using data from
International Economic Databank, Australian National University,
Canberra, July 1992.

Chart 2(b)
Share of Trade, 1990

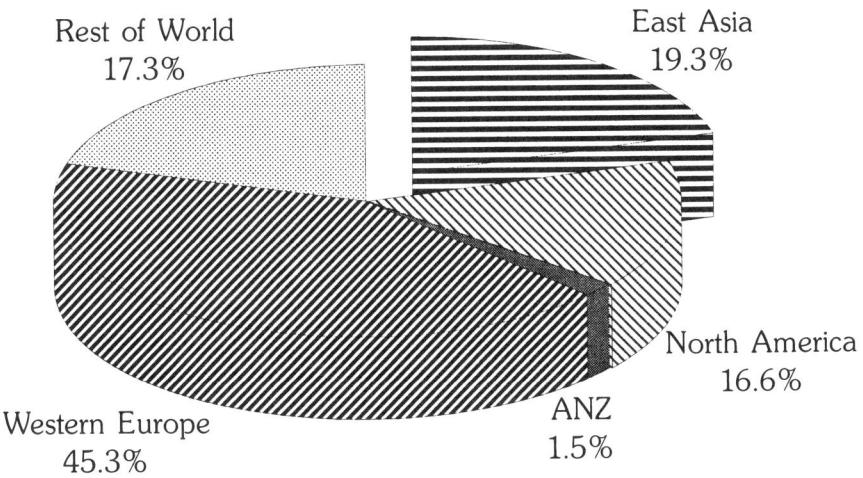

SOURCE: Projections by Australia-Japan Research Centre using para-
meters of output growth and trade intensities calculated using data from
International Economic Databank, Australian National University,
Canberra, July 1992.

Chart 2(c)
Share of Trade, 2000

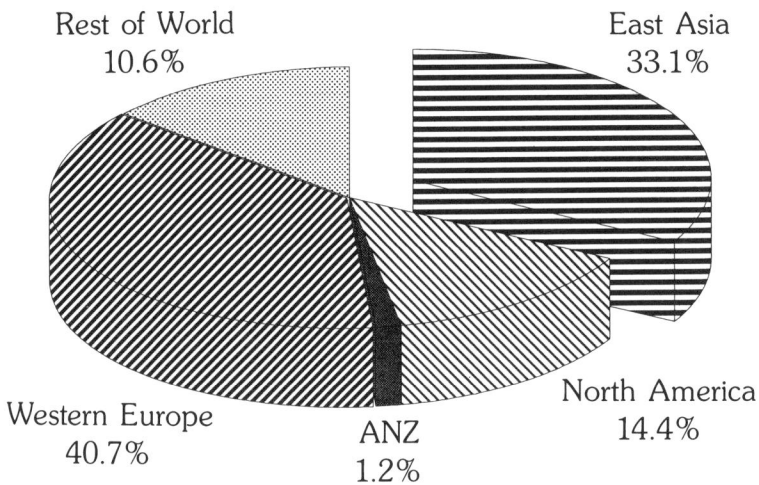

Rest of World
10.6%

East Asia
33.1%

Western Europe
40.7%

ANZ
1.2%

North America
14.4%

SOURCE: Projections by Australia-Japan Research Centre using para-
meters of output growth and trade intensities calculated using data from
International Economic Databank, Australian National University,
Canberra, July 1992.

comprehension that each country's own success in inter-nationally-oriented economic growth depends on its own trade liberalization.

While East Asian developing economies have shown in recent years that they can grow strongly through recession in Japan as well as other advanced industrial economies, there are nevertheless anxieties about the sustainability of growth on the pattern of the recent past. Whilst the region's developing economies have been able to grow strongly despite recession in Japan, they have benefited from con-tinued Japanese industrial transformation, and expansion of direct foreign investment and imports in sectors which have been losing competitiveness. It is reasonable to wonder whether productive industrial transformation will continue indefinitely if there is slow economic recovery in Japan, especially if the political system becomes more open to popular pressure. There is also a question about the sustain-ability of high growth in China, which has been important to continued expansion in the NIEs and other ASEAN economies, under the dual pressures of domestic macro-economic instability and uncertainty about external market access.

The implications of recession in Japan for the regional economy and global economic management are important. The present is significantly different from previous recessions in the post-war period — there will be no export-led recovery as there has been in the past, if only because of the large appreciation of the yen. Nevertheless, the fundamentals of the Japanese economy are strong. The core industrial economy in Japan is in good shape, employment remains high, inflation is low. Japan's strong budget position, very high savings rate, and massive trade and current account surpluses allow further steps to expand domestic demand, and thereby to encourage a recovery that is immediately helpful to export expansion in other countries.

Political uncertainty in Japan will attenuate the process of recovery. The probability of a "double dip" into recession is now high, as the effects of initial fiscal stimulus wear off, while the yen appreciation dampens export growth and inhibits expansion of business investment. However, there is an opportunity for further fiscal stimulus, and it is likely that growth in the order of 3 per cent will be re-established before too long, and retained as a feature of the Japanese economy for the remainder of the decade, despite aging of the Japanese population and social change affecting attitudes to work and leisure.

The change in China is massive and unprecedentedly rapid, both in economic and political terms, and the commitment to reform in China has become more, not less, deeply entrenched since 1989. China is responding increasingly like a market economy; undergoing industrial transformation in a matter which has many parallels to the historical experience of other East Asian nations.

The macro-economic stabilization problems of a partly-reformed economic system in China are formidable. There will be bumps in the road, one of the biggest yet over the year ahead, as yet another inflationary boom is brought to heal.

There is little doubt, however, about the strength of average rates of Chinese economic growth over the medium and longer term. Now that international economic integration has begun, supported by the progressive strengthening of the knowledge and institutions that are necessary for a market economy, the momentum of growth is formidable.

The Chinese are comparing their own and their economy's performances by the high standards of East Asia. They are absorbing rapidly the management and production methods, and the attitudes to economic growth, that have been so productive elsewhere. There are strong pressures to shift the frontier of internationally-oriented growth inland from East and South China, opening the possibility of one or two generations of rapid growth before scarcity and rising costs of labour slows the process.

Getting the framework right for accommodating China now is central to the future management of the global economy and polity. This is a huge challenge for the Asia-Pacific region as China's integration into the international economy moves forward rapidly. It is also a central, if not the central, political security interest in the Asia-Pacific region.

The ASEAN group has also developed its own growth momentum, most importantly with the entrenchment of export-oriented industrialization in indonesia since the mid-1980s. This has been boosted as Korea, Taiwan, and Hong Kong have approached world industrial productivity frontiers and shed standard technology production to China and the ASEAN countries.

There have been signs over the past two years of the direct investment flow to ASEAN diminishing with the greater attraction of China, but momentum in Southeast Asia remains considerable. The industrial transformation of the NIEs has supported and magnified continued upgrading of the technological sophistication and human capital intensity of Japanese production and exports has facilitated the industrial transformation of the NIEs, and accelerated the transfer of labour-intensive processes and industries into mainland China and the ASEAN economies.

19

International investment within the Asia-Pacific economy has expanded even more rapidly than trade. The resulting relocation of production in line with changing industrial structures has led to the emergence of zones of production which transcend political boundaries. Perhaps the best example is the integrated zone of production in South China around Hong Kong; links are also strengthening across the Taiwan Straits, as well as across the Yellow Sea, and between Singapore and its neighbours. These sub-regional integrative processes are market-driven, with government assisting with the physical and intangible infrastructure of commercial exchange but with little formal involvement in a regulatory sense. They are evolving to promote efficiency and competitiveness in global as well as domestic markets, rather than seeking to create a sheltered, discriminatory, sub-regional market.

# V THE WESTERN PACIFIC TRADE MODEL

Until recently, any assessment of the sustainability of East Asian growth would have been made with a strong qualification about its vulnerability to weakness in the international trading system. However, this may not necessarily be the case — that is, so long as East Asian states build constructively on the model of trade policy and expansion that has emerged since the mid-1980s. Over this time, The large majority of East Asian export growth has been to markets in East Asia itself. This is an important reason why strong growth was sustained in East Asian developing countries through the recession in the industrial countries.

It goes without saying that the opportunities for East Asian growth are greater if the markets of Europe and North America are expanding, and remaining open to increased volumes of intercontinental trade. But these influences on East Asian growth are becoming steadily less critical, as the scale of East Asian production and trade expands. It is now open to East Asia to consider continued commitment to multilateral open trade as the basis of a high growth strategy, even if the United States is unsympathetic to open trade, and remains aloof. This is a new element in Asia-Pacific economic relations, to which the political economy of trade policy will take some time to adjust on both sides of the Pacific.

The East Asian economies have in fact, and contrary to popular perception in the United States and Europe, undertaken more trade and economic liberalization in the last two decades than any other group of countries.

The reality of East Asian and Asia-Pacific regional trade expansion is very different from that which is emerging in North America and which is established and continuing to develop in Europe.

There has been no economically important trade-expanding discrimination in East Asia. Trade preferences within the Association of Southeast Asian Nations (ASEAN) region so far have had trivial effects, although the 1991 commitment by Heads of Government to move towards an ASEAN Free Trade Area (AFTA) will have future significance. The two most rapidly expanding intra-East Asian bilateral trading relationships over the past several years — between mainland China and Taiwan, and China and the Republic of Korea — have developed around and despite discriminatory restrictions on bilateral trade. Trade discrimination in Australia-New Zealand and North America has been associated with relatively small parts of the total Asia-Pacific trade expansion.

East Asian and Asia-Pacific trade expansion has nevertheless been associated with reductions in barriers to international trade, including intraregional trade. All Western Pacific member economies of APEC except Hong Kong and Singapore have substantially reduced official border restrictions over the past decade, especially since the mid-1980s. Hong Kong and Singapore have, throughout the period under discussion, been the world's most important examples of free trading economies. There has been major import liberalization in Japan, Korea, Taiwan, mainland China, Thailand, Malaysia, Indonesia, Australia, and New Zealand. Political weakness has meant that the Philippines has made slower progress, although recent official commitments are impressive. Trade liberalization has been mostly non-discriminatory and unilateral, and sometimes influenced by the multilateral disciplines of GATT. The main exceptions, sometimes temporary, have favoured the United States, following pressure from that country to reduce bilateral trade imbalances. Even more important has been the reduction of non-official barriers to trade of many kinds, in the process of deep integration into the international economy.

The new model of regional and international trade expansion which has developed in the Asia-Pacific, and especially in the Western Pacific economies, is consistent with the spirit of GATT as it was conceived in the 1940s and as it developed in the early post-war decades. Three crucial features distinguish Asia-Pacific trade expansion and take it beyond GATT's Constitution, rules and practice, and beyond

GATT's framework for the encouragement of regional trade expansion under Article XXIV.

The first distinguishing feature derives from the fact that GATT negotiations in practice have assumed that liberalization is a concession, the withholding of which has value for a member country. The trade negotiations "game" within GATT therefore has elements of the prisoner's dilemma, in which, in the absence of deliberate communication and co-operation, the outcome is the least favourable for each participating country. In contrast, the trade expansion "game" that has emerged in the Western Pacific can be characterized as "prisoner's delight". Observing the highly beneficial effect of an individual country's liberalization on its own trade expansion, each Western Pacific country has determined that, whatever the policies of others, it will benefit more from keeping its own borders open than from seeking protection. Each country's liberalization in its own interests has increased the benefits that trading partners receive from their own liberalization. This "prisoner's delight" game thus involves a series of movements towards sets of trade-policy initiatives that are more favourable for all countries. Of course, there are gaps and exceptions which reflect the domestic political economy of industry policy in most economies, the most notable being Northeast Asian agriculture. It is with respect to such exceptions that pressure from outside plays an important role in each country's trade liberalization, so far most effectively through multilateral negotiations and other forums of GATT, but sometimes in bilateral negotiations influenced by GATT disciplines (see Garnaut 1991; Drysdale and Garnaut 1992).

The payoffs from unilateral trade liberalization, across the range of trade-policy stances of other countries that generate the "prisoner's delight", are recognizable as the outcomes predicted in standard trade theory. What is new in East Asia and the Western Pacific is that close observation in neighbouring country after neighbouring country that trade liberalization enhances economic performance has changed political perceptions of the payoff matrix. Any perceived disadvantages in changes in income distribution associated with trade liberalization are judged by the political process to be less important than national gains. Those judgements are helped by the obviously favourable effects on the incomes of the relatively poor of labour-intensive manufactured export expansion in labour-abundant economies.

The second distinguishing feature of Asia-Pacific trade expansion is that it has not been associated with substantial discrimination in trade policy. Official barriers have not been lower for intra-regional than extra-regional trade expansion.

Third, the East Asian and Pacific experience demonstrates powerfully the importance of non-official barriers to trade and the role that their reduction plays in trade expansion and economic development.

A major strategic interest for East Asian and Western Pacific countries is thus to sustain the process of open trade and economic liberalization through GATT and to counter tendencies towards closed regionalism. This was the context of East Asia's commitment to the Uruguay Round. While there is a natural apprehension about developments in North America (NAFTA) and Europe, reflected in Malaysian Prime Minister Mahathir's proposal for a new East Asian Economic Group (EAEG, now called East Asian Economic Caucus or EAEC), the framework of APEC and its inclusion of the world's two largest economic powers provides a powerful instrument for containing inclinations towards inward-looking policy developments in the Pacific region and elsewhere.

It is precisely these interests which led to the establishment of the Asia-Pacific mechanisms for communicating policy interests and priorities, both to exploit the potential for trade and economic growth in a very rapidly changing regional economy, and to project and define East Asian and Pacific responsibilities in the global arena.

East Asian and Pacific trading links are especially strong. In 1992, APEC economies accounted for 75 per cent of each other's trade, but only for 44 per cent of world trade. Intra-East Asian trade accounts for 45 per cent of these economies' exports (see Drysdale and Garnaut 1993, for discussion of the relationship of these ratios to *intensity* of trade).

Expanding trade amongst APEC economies has continued to involve North America and Australasia, and not only East Asia. East Asian trade with the Northeast and Southwest Pacific has, however, grown more slowly than intra-East Asian trade, reflecting the slower growth of those regions.

North America's share in East Asia's markets fell rapidly with declining competitiveness and the increased role of oil imports through the 1970s, but steadied through the 1990s. Its share in Japan's imports responded significantly to improved competitiveness (and a lower price of oil) from the mid-1980s (Chart 3). Australasia's share of East Asian markets followed a similar pattern, although it was diminished by low commodity prices in recent years (Chart 4).

Neither North America nor Australasia held import share as well in East Asia as a whole as in Japan, reflecting the

# Chart 3
## North America's Share in East Asia's and Japan's Imports, 1970-92
### (In percentages)

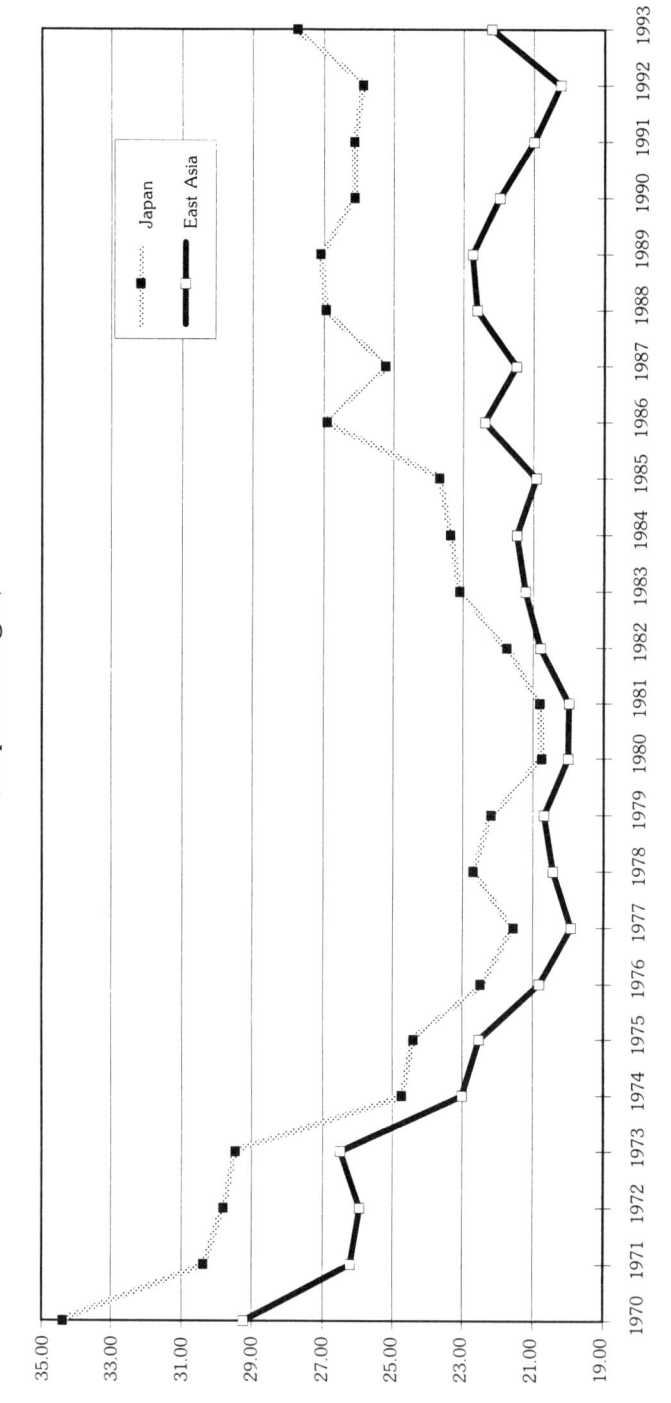

SOURCE: Australia-Japan Research Centre, International Economic Databank, compiled from United Nations and International Monetary Fund statistics.

# Chart 4

## Australasia's Share in East Asia's and Japan's Imports, 1970-92

### (In percentages)

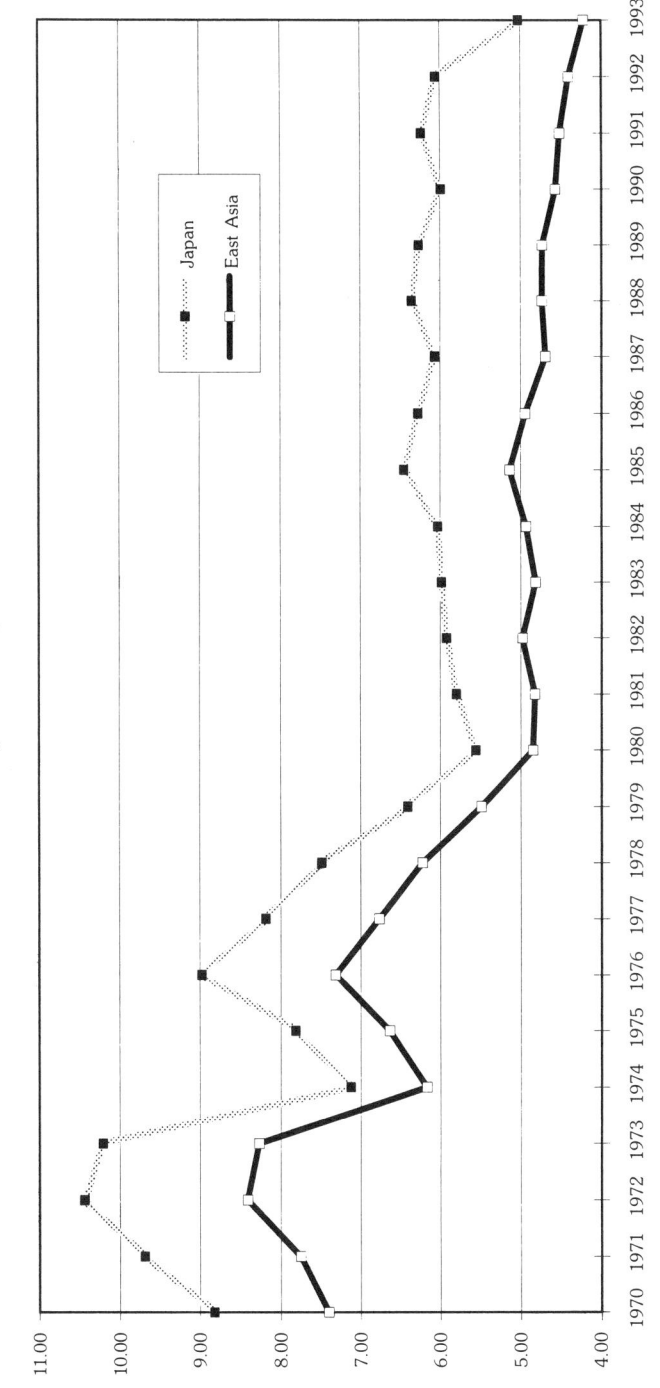

SOURCE: Australia-Japan Research Centre, International Economic Databank, compiled from United Nations and International Monetary Fund statistics.

explosive growth of intra-regional trade amongst developing East Asian economies, most importantly involving China.

Both North America and Australasia can draw lessons from variations in export performance to East Asia over the past two decades. The lesson is that, whatever the perception of official or institutional barriers to trade, their export performance is highly responsive to their own economies' international competitiveness. This limits the scope for passing blame for weaknesses in export performance in East Asian markets onto others.

The North American export performance in Japanese and East Asian markets through the 1980s is surprising in the light of the pessimistic tone of American public discussion, and of the domestic policy inhibitions to international competitiveness. In particular, the United States and Canada have continued to carry the burden of loose public budgets. The most significant initiative of the Clinton Administration thus far, has been to put in train a legislative process to re-align fiscal policy, offering the prospect of stronger domestic investment, and sustainable improvement in competitiveness and the current account. Success in this initiative, and increasing U.S. awareness of the strength of its export performance, could ease the domestic political pressures on trans-Pacific relations.

At the same time, North America and Australasia have become proportionately much less important, and East Asia much more important, as destinations for exports since 1986 (Charts 5, 6 and 7). More rapidly than is generally understood in the United States, the North American market has become less crucial to overall export performance in East Asia. Before many more years have passed, this geo-economic reality will have an important effect on the

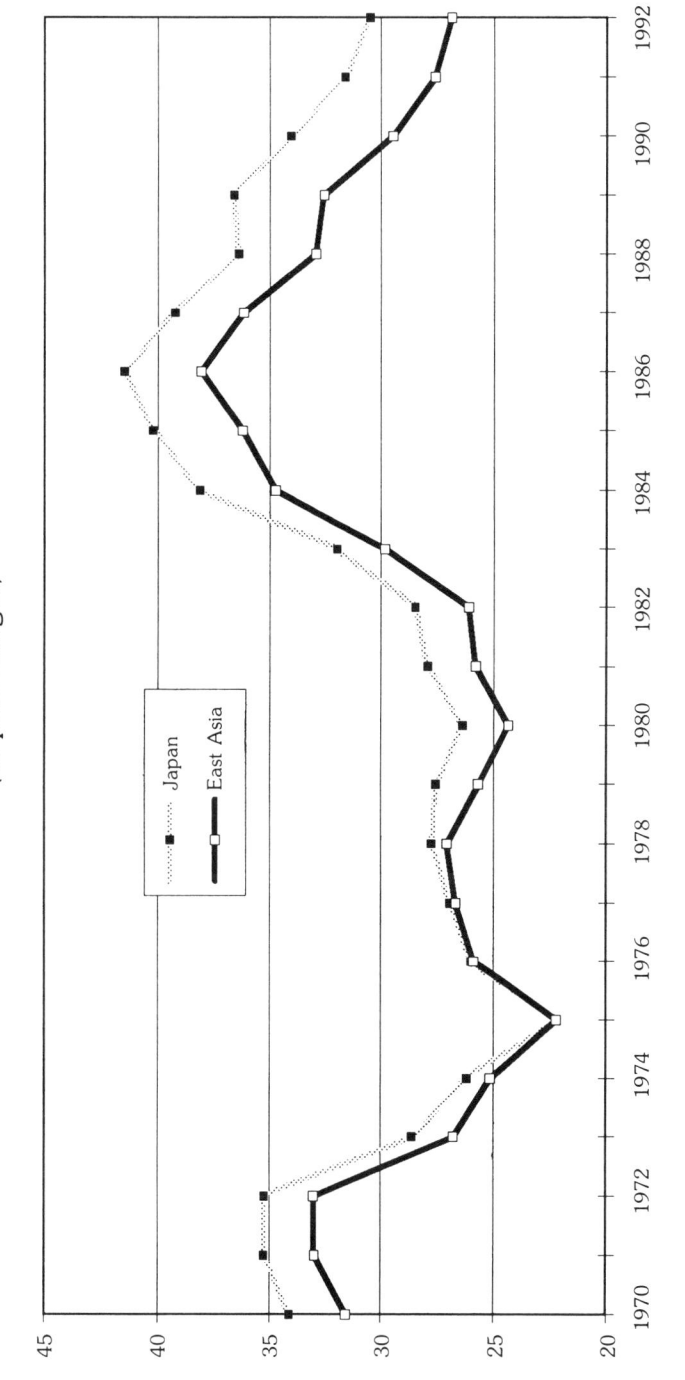

Chart 5

North America's Share in East Asia's and Japan's Exports, 1970–92

(In percentages)

SOURCE: Australia-Japan Research Centre, International Economic Databank, compiled from United Nations and Inter-national Monetary Fund statistics.

# Chart 6

## Australasia's Share in East Asia's and Japan's Exports, 1970-92
### (In percentages)

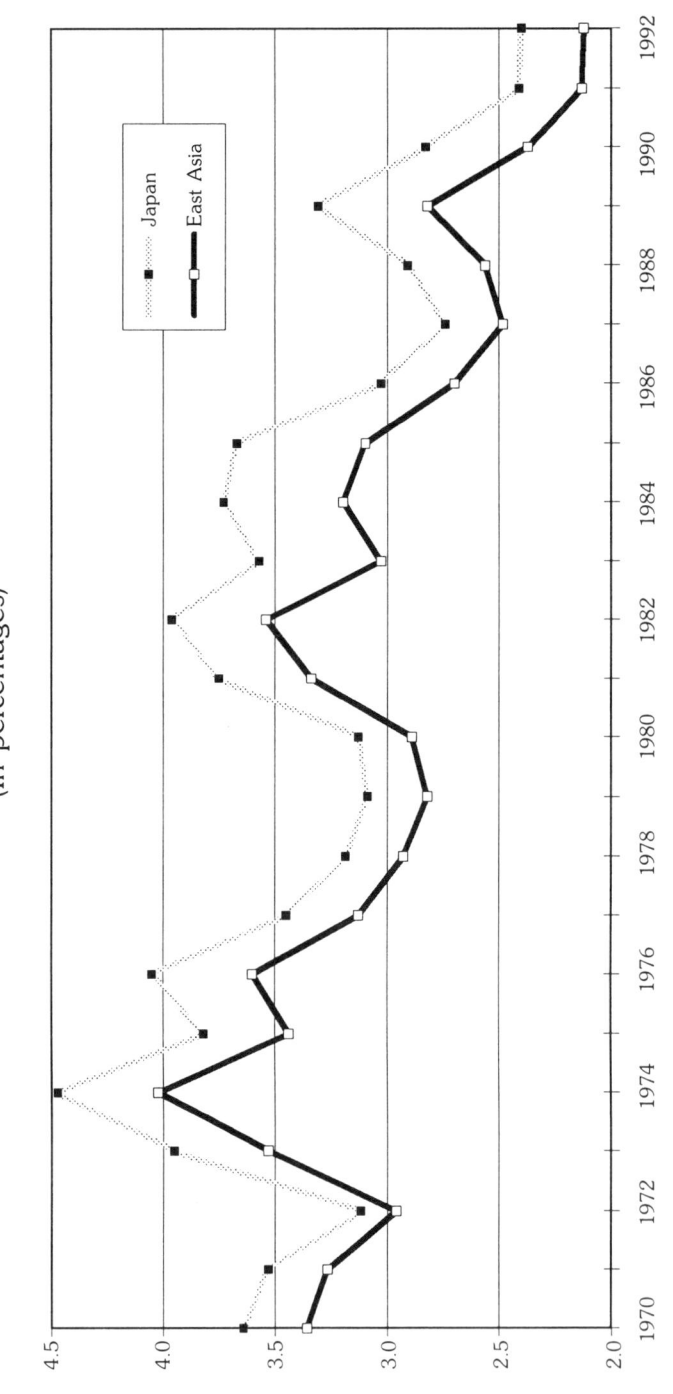

SOURCE: Australia-Japan Research Centre, International Economic Databank, compiled from United Nations and International Monetary Fund statistics.

# Chart 7

## East Asia's Share in East Asia's Exports and Imports, 1970–92

### (In percentages)

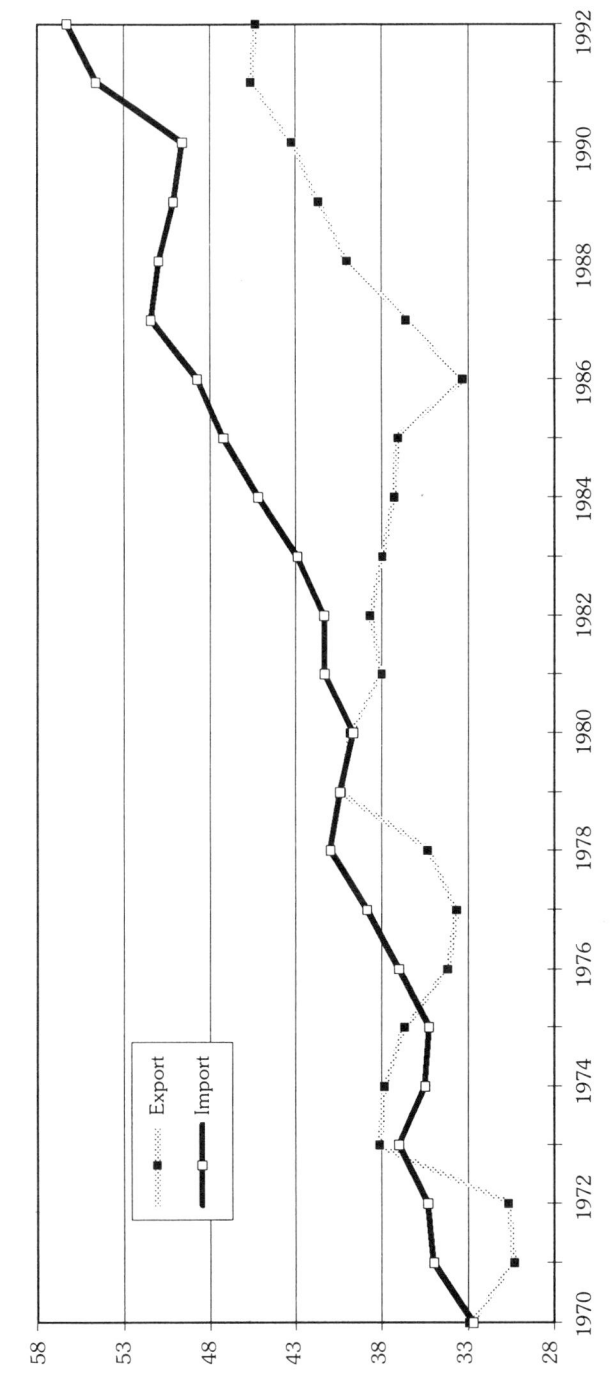

SOURCE: Australia-Japan Research Centre, International Economic Databank, compiled from United Nations and International Monetary Fund statistics.

extent to which East Asian states are prepared to accommodate the idiosyncrasies of U.S. policy-making processes.

Underpinning this challenge is the importance of getting the policy framework right to sustain industrial and trade integration in East Asia and continued growth of market opportunities in the region. The continuation of the game of "prisoner's delight" — mutually beneficial trade liberalization in the region — cannot be taken for granted. It has proceeded rapidly over the past few decades. It will continue if barriers to deeper integration in the region are negotiated in a framework that creates confidence in the process, not tension and uncertainty. Trade arrangements which introduce discrimination by some regional economies against others could create serious divisions within the region. The "invitation", by the Bush Administration, in its unsuccessful re-election campaign, for individual Western Pacific economies to form separate, preferential trading agreements with the United States will, hopefully, never be reiterated, for it threatened to reintroduce the ideas into the region that have created the traditional trade policy "prisoner's dilemma": leading each country, in narrow and ultimately mistaken pursuit of its own self interest, through insisting on reciprocity and excluding outsiders, to take steps that make all worse off.

This means developing a favourable policy environment. But it also means establishing a mechanism for effective communication of policy interests and priorities, to exploit the potential for further economic growth and intra-regional trade in this dynamic part of the world, and to project and define East Asian and Pacific interests and responsibilities in the global arena.

As the centre of the world's economic gravity has shifted

towards East Asia and the Pacific, shared interest in fostering Asia-Pacific integration, based on the principles and policy objectives of *open regionalism*, has become more powerful.


# VI OPEN REGIONALISM: FRAMEWORK FOR ASIA-PACIFIC ECONOMIC CO-OPERATION

The essential requirements of economic co-operation in the Asia-Pacific region are: *openness* in international economic policy and diplomatic approach; *evolution* in the practice of high-level consultation and cooperation; and *non-discrimination* in growing economic partnership among disparate polities (Yamazawa 1992).

The Pacific Economic Co-operation Council (PECC), established in 1980, was the first building block in the architecture of regional economic policy consultation. PECC — with its informal, tripartite structure, which includes participation at the official, industry and academic level — carried forward the process of fostering consultation and discussion of interests in regional co-operation through its trade policy forum and other task forces.

An important policy achievement which grew out of consultations within PECC was the development of Asia-Pacific support for the Uruguay Round of multilateral trade negotiations, and the facilitation of broader economic dialogue involving both China and Taiwan. PECC's semi-official processes also laid the groundwork for the next step in the development of outward-looking economic co-operation — the evolution of the Asia-Pacific Economic Co-operation

(APEC) group. APEC, through the establishment of regular ministerial-level meetings, brought the process of economic co-operation into the political arena.

APEC was established at ministerial level in 1989, and has rapidly established itself as the main regional forum for discussion of trade liberalization and expansion.

APEC has fostered consistency between regional economic policy objectives and multilateral international economic policy goals — and sought to strengthen the GATT-based multilateral trading system.

APEC could pursue these objectives most effectively if it were able to set positive examples of successful trade liberalization and expansion. It is imperative that any joint economic or trade policy decisions by APEC be consistent with the fundamental principle of universal *most-favoured-nation* treatment of all trading partners as set out in Article I of GATT. This contrasts with joint decisions that explicitly discriminate against non-participants, and seek to rationalize discrimination by reference to Article XXIV. Any attempt to negotiate an APEC-wide preferential trading agreement would be economically undesirable, given the trade and investment links of the East Asian and ASEAN economies outside the region, especially with the EC: it would also be destined to end in failure.

Discriminatory trade amongst APEC members would have the additional and major drawback that it would place artificial barriers in the path of the entrenchment of internationally-oriented growth in South Asia and Indochina. It would contrast with the deepening of non-discriminatory trade liberalization and expansion in the Western Pacific in recent years, which has contributed to a highly favourable environment for the participation of the emerging market economies of the region, to the benefit of old and new players alike.

If APEC is to establish itself as a promoter of open and multilateral trade, it must remain an *open economic association*:

- *open* in the sense of not discriminating against the rest of the world;
- *economic* in its primary policy focus;
- an *association* in the sense of seeking voluntary understandings on principles and policy action that yield benefits to all participants, rather than imposing a supra-national authority on participants.

The biggest danger for Asia-Pacific economic expansion and political security is that the Pacific, under stress, might split down the middle. Regionalism and protectionism in North America and Europe invite a regionalist East Asian response, but a split makes no economic or political sense. That is one of the reasons why it is so important for Australia, Japan, and other Western Pacific countries to articulate a clear and constructive response to the drift in trans-Pacific tensions. That is one reason why strong commitment to the APEC framework for regional economic dealings is so important, because it encompasses both North American and Western Pacific economic and political interests and provides a vehicle for dealing with them in the post-Cold War period. The APEC framework of open regionalism is conducive to the successful completion of the Uruguay Round, and to the continued viability of the multilateral system following the negotiations.

The North American Free Trade Agreement (NAFTA) if passed into law will appear less threatening to traders and investors outside North America if the Uruguay Round is completed successfully, if natfa can be engaged in open Asia-Pacific regionalism, and if bilateral tensions between North America and East Asia can be settled within this multilateral framework.

The framework of APEC and its inclusion of the world's two largest economic powers provides a powerful instrument for containing inclinations towards inward-looking policy developments. The successful development of open regionalism in the Asia-Pacific region would provide a supportive framework for the European Community to move back to support of open, multilateral trade if, and when, the dissipation of the EC's current mode of introversion allows. It is as likely a mechanism as the world now has to provide urgently needed leadership in an open approach to global economic affairs.

# VII CHALLENGES FOR THE FUTURE

As rapid economic growth has changed the structure of world economic power, it has challenged the old definition of political and security interests in East Asia and the Pacific in the post-Cold War era. With the end of American economic Hegemony, new regional and multilateral political structures are needed to define rules governing the relations between Asia-Pacific states, provide a framework for the emerging strategic significance of Japan and China, and ASEAN, and establish a forum for discussing a wide range of regional and sub-regional security issues.

U.S.-Japan economic tensions are more likely to be manageable if the established framework of security relations remains intact. The United States — a strong stabilizing factor in regional security — is more likely to maintain a presence in the Western Pacific if there is a strong enough economic rationale for it.

In political as well as in economic affairs, the pace of change must encourage experimentation with new structures to manage regional and sub-regional problems. To reflect the impact of economic policy on political and security arrangements, the aim should not be to develop a single over-arching regional structure dealing with economic, political and security issues. Rather, separate structures are more realistic, but to be successful they need to reinforce each other.

# VIII CONCRETE STEPS

The challenge is to make the Asia-Pacific economy a source of strength for a liberal international system, and to encourage regional trade expansion without discriminating against non-regional nations. Despite the well-known limitations of GATT's most-favoured-nation based trade rules, they constrain the political threat of discrimination and provide a measure of security and political confidence in open international economic transactions.

Completing the unfinished business of the Uruguay Round is urgent. Yet, from the perspective of Western Pacific economies, the Uruguay Round is not the end of trade policy history, but the beginning, since it coincides with the region's continuing implementation of substantial reform and economic liberalization programmes within the region. APEC is of critical importance in defining the international trade and economic policy agenda beyond the Uruguay Round.

This is obviously a very important year for APEC. With the United States in the chair, and therefore with a strong interest in defining a substantial agenda for regional co-operation and negotiation, this is a time for laying out a long-term strategy for Asia-Pacific economic co-operation. The next APEC meeting is due to be held in Seattle in November. If the vexed question of participation by the People's Republic of China can be settled alongside representation from Taipei, this meeting will be the first attended by government leaders from most APEC economies. It will focus corporate attention and energies on regional developments.[*]

There are four central policy interests in Asia-Pacific economic co-operation:

- Maintaining support for the "Western Pacific trade model", within the region, especially through communications that give each economy confidence that its partners will continue down this path;
- Engaging North America in Asia-Pacific *open regionalism*;
- Defining an agenda of strengthening the "public goods" that facilitate trade. The measures covered by this agenda can profitably include region-wide understanding on rules for foreign investment; enhanced efficiency and compatibility in the provision of tangible international public goods such as transport and communications infrastructure; mutual recognition of standards; greater harmonization of legal and administration procedures; and effective

---

[*] See Postscript for an update on the November 1993 APEC Meeting.

means of resolving potential disputes. Issues such as these are at the heart of North American economic interests in Asia-Pacific co-operation and the Western Pacific interest in deeper economic integration;

• In the longer term, negotiating new packages of trade liberalization on unconditional most-favoured nation terms, including on a sectoral basis, that go beyond Uruguay Round outcomes.

It is also critical that APEC supports confidence in China's commitment to outward-looking economic policies and political development. An urgent task is the full participation of both China and Taiwan in GATT.

The process of sorting out these priorities is underway within PECC and APEC's Eminent Persons Group.

In February 1993, Australian Prime Minister Paul Keating suggested an Asia-Pacific Framework Agreement under which these issues might be addressed over a period of time. This could provide the foundations for an Asia-Pacific Economic Community, an open economic association of regional economies, based on the principles of open regionalism. It would incidentally provide opportunities for European, South Asian and Indochinese trade expansion — to the APEC region's benefit — thereby making some contribution to the carrying of Europe's eastern burden and challenging Europe to join the Asia-Pacific economies in the next round of trade liberalization and expansion in the second half of the 1990s.

Progress along these lines in Seattle in November, or in Indonesia in 1995, would allow more ambitious steps to be attempted within the framework of open regionalism. It would be highly advantageous if APEC members were then able to discuss liberalization of trade in sectors of major importance to each other, extending Uruguay Round outcomes to some non-participants, and going beyond them where practicable. Developing strategies to negotiate a package of liberalization measures within the APEC framework, such as for agricultural products, in the textile and steel industries, and alignment of trade-expanding institutions, will be complex, and must build on success in simpler forms of co-operation within the APEC framework.

It now seems that the historic mission of East Asia and the Western Pacific in the international system is to sustain appreciation of the superiority of a multilateral framework of open trade. APEC has become the immediate arena of contests between discriminatory and multilateral versions of open trade. If the Western Pacific holds APEC to its recently but firmly established course, it will strengthen the sustainability of open trade on a global basis. It will have answered the challenge of the international environment to the Asian market economies.

# POSTSCRIPT DECEMBER 1993

In the last two months of 1993, the regional and international context of Asia-Pacific economic growth has come together in a favourable way, as a result of three major events: the passage of the NAFTA arrangements through the United States Congress; the successful meeting of APEC Heads of Government in Seattle; and the successful completion of the Uruguay Round.

While NAFTA in itself has undesirable features, by 1993 its passage through the Congress had become an essential condition for the United States administration holding the line on inward-looking tendencies in the national polity. Victory in the Congress gave outward-looking elements of the Clinton Administration confidence and momentum that was important to success in the APEC leaders meeting and the final stages of the Uruguay Round negotiations.

The undesirable features of NAFTA include its embodiment of trade discrimination under Article XXIV of GATT, and additional distortions associated with unwieldy rules of origin.

For East Asia, NAFTA always presented substantial problems. Trade and investment diversion raised concerns in East Asian countries. But to East Asia, the direct damage was less important than the larger threat NAFTA posed to the international trading system. Within Southeast Asia, the United States discussion of NAFTA was a trigger for Malaysian Prime Minister Mahathir's idea of an East Asian Economic Caucus (EAEC), and for commitment to the ASEAN Free Trade Area (AFTA).

As 1993 drew towards a close, however, the reservations in East Asia and the Western Pacific about the dangers of NAFTA were overwhelmed as the Clinton Administration faced the test of getting NAFTA through Congress, and East Asia considered the impact of his possible failure upon the constituency for open trade in North Aemrica. Western Pacific reservations about NAFTA were used as it became clear that its main proponents within the administration saw NAFTA in a wider context that included commitments to trade facilitation among APEC countries and to the success-ful conclusion of the Uruguay Round.

The conjuncture of the NAFTA decision and the APEC meetings in Seattle presented an important opportunity for reconciling new directions in Washington with concerns and ambitions in East Asian countries. It was an historic opportunity for setting trade and international economic diplomacy on a sound new course.

There was significant progress towards building co-operative efforts and a new kind of Asia-Pacific economic community in Seattle. The focus on the short-term objective of putting pressure on completion of the Uruguay Round was sharp and effective, especially because Japan and the United States, whose leaders came to the meetings with new polit-ical authority, established effective common cause.

On the longer term agenda, effective attention was also given to the priority of trade and investment facilitation measures and building the infrastructure for deeper economic integration in the region. These measures will enhance the prospects for trade and investment expansion, and hence rapid economic growth in the region, as well as accelerate active co-operation and institution-building among the members of APEC.

Yet a major strategic objective of the APEC meetings, to commit APEC nations to the long-term goal of free trade and openness in the international economy, appears to have been fumbled.

East Asian members rejected commitment to the idea of an Asian-Pacific Economic Community because they were uncomfortable with the particular vision of free trade with which it came to be associated as a result of some mainly American advocacy — a tight discriminatory economic bloc. This was not mere semantics.

In the preparation for APEC, within the Eminent Persons Group (EPG), who were charged with defining an agenda for the future, the choice between an agenda based on co-operative efforts at trade facilitation and non-discriminatory trade liberalization and an agenda based on development, in some circumstance or other, of a discriminatory regional free trade area, was a hotly contested issue. The East Asians rejected the latter vision which the United States had earlier proposed. In the final EPG document ambiguity persisted.

That ambiguity infected the approach of ministers and leaders to the constructive reconciliation of agendas on each side of the Pacific.

In fact there was no rejection of a free trade agenda for Asia and the Pacific at Seattle. But there was decisive rejection of any notion of an exclusionary bloc.

This confirms as reality a perception that has emerged

strongly in recent years in the Western Pacific: the only kind of Asia-Pacific economic community that will work is one that engages the disparate membership of APEC (including Malaysia) in a new kind of economic community, promoting liberalization through co-operative endeavours, not through closed and discriminatory policy measures on the EC and NAFTA pattern — an exemplar of non-discriminatory *open regionalism*, and a force for promoting an open international economic system.

Amongst a huge success for Asia-Pacific co-operation, this one message Seattle faled to deliver exactly on cue. The message eventually came through clearly. It is a message that is crucial to the continuation of successful East Asian industrial transformation and Western Pacific global economic interests. It is also crucial to political security, as frustration of legitimate economic ambitions in East Asia would encourage and aggravate political introversion and uncertainty. It is a message that is at the heart of APEC's future success.

The leaders' meeting planned for Jakarta next year provides the best opportunity to get this right. Indonesian leadership will be helpful to elaborating a vision which allows APEC's already considerable momentum to grow, centripetally, around the concept of *open regionalism* which has emerged from the long dialogue among Western Pacific countries on these issues.

The APEC leaders' meeting provided the opportunity for re-establishing high-level contact between the governments of China and the United States, and was part of the increasing realism in U.S. management of the China relationship in the second half of 1993. It also provided a favourable context for embedding new, more open trends that emerged in the United States' perception of and management of relations with Japan through this period.

The APEC message on multilateral trade was one element in the increased momentum of Uruguay Round negotiations, that led to the successful outcome on 15 December 1993.

The year 1993 began with an inexperienced U.S. administration inheriting a political situation that contained growing tendencies to protectionism and regionalism. Its inexperience and its misperception of East Asia, especially Japanese and Chinese, reality, raised the political temperature and threatened to corrode the basis of co-operative relations across the North Pacific.

As the year ends, these dangerous tendencies have been placed firmly within an Asian Pacific and multilateral framework of open economic relations that substantially diminish the dangers.

# REFERENCES

Anderson, Kym. "Europe 1992 and the Western Pacific Economies". *Economic Journal* 101 (November 1992).

Anderson, Kym and Hege Norheim. *Is World Trade Becoming More Regionalised?* Geneva: General Agreement on Tariffs and Trade Secretariat, 1992.

Balassa, Bela. "Japan's Trade Policies". *Weltwirtschaftliches Archiv* 122, no. 4 (1986).

Bergsten, C. Fred and Marcus Noland. *Reconcilable Differences? United States-Japan Economic Conflict*. Washington D.C.: Institute for International Economics, 1993.

Bhagwati, Jagdish. "Regionalism vs. Multilateralism: An Overview". Paper presented at the World BankCPER Conference on New Dimensions in Regional Integration. Washington, 2-3 April 1992.

Cooper, Richard. *Worldwide Versus Regional Integration: Is There an Optimal Size of the Integrated Area?* Yale: Economic Growth Center Discussion Paper, no. 220, November 1974.

Drysdale, Peter. *International Economic Pluralism: Economic*

*Policy in East Asia and the Pacific*. New York, Columbia University Press, and Sydney: Allen and Unwin, 1988.

Drysdale, Peter. *Open Regionalism: A Key to East Asia's Economic Future*. Pacific Economic Papers no. 197. Canberra: Australia-Japan Research Centre, Australia National University, July 1991.

_____. "The challenge of open economic integration in the Asia Pacific". Paper presented to the Japan America Society of Chicago, Fourth Chicago Symposium, Economic Regionalism in the Pacific, 22–24 July 1993.

_____. "The Proposal for an East Asian Steel Community". Paper presented at the Fourth Global Contribution Seminar on the Asia-Pacific's Further Development and Ongoing Global Economic Growth, Tokyo, 1–5 June 1993.

Drysdale, Peter and Andrew Elek. *China and the International Trading System*. Pacific Economic Papers no. 214. Canberra: Australia-Japan Research Centre, Australian National University, December 1992.

Drysdale, Peter and Ross Garnaut. "Trade Intensities and the Analysis of Bilateral Trade Flows in a Many-Country World". *Hitotsubashi Journal of Economics* 22, no. 2 (February 1982).

_____. "A Pacific Free Trade Area?" In *More Free Trade Area?* edited by Jeffrey J. Schott. Policy Analysis in International Economics, no. 27. Washington: Institute of International Economics, 1989.

_____. "NAFTA and the Pacific Region: Strategic Responses". Paper presented at the Conference on the Implications of the North American Free Trade Agreement, Adelaide University, July 1992.

_____. "The Pacific: An Application of a General Theory of Economic Integration". In *Pacific Dynamism and the International Economic System*, edited by C.F. Bergsten and M. Noland. Washington D.C.: Institute for International Economics, 1993.

Elek, Andrew. "Pacific Economic Cooperation: Policy Choices for the 1990s". *Asia Pacific Economic Literature* 6, no. 1 (May 1992*a*).

_____. "Trade Policy Options for the Asia Pacific Region in the 1990s: The Potential of Open Regionalism". *American Economic Review* (Papers and Proceedings 32) no. 2 (May 1992*b*).

_____. "Regionalism in the World Economy: Implications for AFTA and ASEAN Trade Policy". Paper prepared for 17th Conference of the Federation of ASEAN Economic Associations, AFTA and Beyond, Surabaya, Indonesia, 15–17 Nofember 1992*c*.

_____. "Asia-Pacific Economic Cooperation: Opportunities and Risks for a New Initiative". Paper prepared for the Asia-Australia Institute, Asia Leaders Forum, APEC in Asia, 28–29 June 1993.

Finger, Michael J. "GATT's Influence on Regional Trade Arrangements". Paper presented at the World BankCPER

Conference on New Dimensions in Regional Integration, Washington, 2–3 April 1992.

Frankel, Jeffrey. "Is a Yen Bloc Forming in Pacific Asia?" In *Finance and the International Economy*, The AMEX Bank Review Prize Essays. Oxford: Oxford University Press, 1991.

_____. "Is Japan Creating a Yen Bloc in East Asia and the Pacific?" Paper presented at the NBER Conference on Japan and the U.S. in Pacific Asia, Del Mar, CA, 3–5 April 1992.

Fukusaku, Kiichiro. *Economic Regionalism and the Intra-Industry Trade: Pacific Asia Perspectives*. Technical Papers no. 53. Paris: OECD Development Centre, February 1992.

Garnaut, Ross. "Australian Trade with Southeast Asia: A Study of Resistances to Bilateral Trade Flows". Doctoral thesis, Australian National University, Canberra, 1972.

_____. "The Market and the State in Economic Development". *Singapore Economic Review* XXXVI, no. 2 (October 1991).

_____. "The Market and the State in Economic Development: Applications to the International System". *Singapore Economic Review*, 1992.

Garnaut, Ross and Guonan Ma. *China's Grain Economy*. Canberra: Australian Government Publishing Service, 1992.

_____. "How Rich is China: Evidence from the Food

Economy". *Australian Journal of Chinese Affairs*, no. 30 (1993), pp. 121-48.

Hughes, Helen. "The Prospects of ASEAN Countries in Industrialised Country Markets". In *ASEAN in ka Changing Pacific and World Economy*, edited by Ross Garnaut. Canberra: Australian National University Press, 1980.

Irwin, Douglas A. "Multilateral and Bilateral Trade Policies in the World Trading System: An Historical Perspective". Paper presented at the World BankCPER Conference on New Dimensions in Regional Integration, Washington, 2-3 April 1992.

James, William E. and Robert McCleary. "The U.S. Response to Increasing Regionalism: A Pacific Perspective". Paper presented at the "Europe and Asia in the 1990s" conference held at the East-West Center, Honolulu, August 1991.

Kojima, Kiyoshi. "Japan and the Future of World Trade Policy". In *Towards a New World Trade Policy: The Maidenhead Papers*, edited by C.F. Bergsten. London: Lexington Books, 1975.

Krugman, Paul. "The Move to Free Trade Zones". *Federal Reserve Bank of Kansas Review*, December 1991.

_____. "Regionalism vs. Multilateralism: Analytical Notes". Paper presented at the World BankCPER Conference on Regional Integration, Washington, 2-3 April 1992.

Lawrence, Robert. *Imports in Japan: Closed Markets or Closed Minds?* Brookings Papers on Economic Activity, no. 2. Washington: The Brookings Institution, 1987.

_____. "How Open is Japan?" In *Trade with Japan: Has the Door Opened Wider?* edited by Paul Krugman. Chicago: University of Chicago Press, 1991.

Lincoln, Edward J. *Japan's Unequal Trade.* Washington: The Brookings Institution, 1990.

Lipsey, R.G. "The Theory of Customs Unions: A General Theory". *The Economic Journal* 70, no. 279 (1960).

Milner, Helen. "A Three Bloc Trading System". Paper presented at the IPSA Conference, Buenos Aires, Argentina, 20-25 July 1991.

Nogues, Julio and Rosalinda Quintanilla. "Latin America's Integration and the Multilateral Trading System". Paper presented at the World BankCPER Conference on New Dimensions in Regional Integration, Washington, 2-3 April 1992.

Noland, Marcus. "Protectionism in Japan". Paper presented for the *Open Economies Review* 4: 67-81. Washington: Institute for International Economics, 1992.

Pacific Basin Economic Council. "North American Free Trade: Implications for International Business". San Francisco: PBEC Secretariat, 1992.

Petri, Peter. "Japanese Trade in Transition: Hypotheses and Recent Evidence". In *Trade with Japan: Has the Door Opened Wider?* edited by Paul Krugman. Chicago: University of Chicago Press, 1991.

Saxonhouse, Gary. "Trading Blocs, Pacific Trade and Pricing Strategies of East Asian Firms". Paper presented at the

World BankCPER Conference on New Dimensions in Regional Integration, Washington, 2-3 April 1992.

Sheard, Paul. *Keiretsu and Closedness of the Japanese Market: An Economic Appraisal.* Discussion Paper no. 273. Osaka: The Institute of Social and Economic Research, Osaka University, June 1992.

Snape, Richard. Paper to the Helen Hughes Festschrift, The Australian National University, August 1993.

Summers, Lawrence H. "Regionalism and the World Trading System". Paper presented at the Kansas Hole Conference on Free Trade Areas, Federal Reserve Bank of Kansas City, August 1991.

Sung Yun-Wing. "The Economic Integration of Hong Kong, Taiwan and South Korea with the Mainland of China". In *Economic Reform and Internationalisation: China and the Pacific Region*, edited by Ross Garnaut and Liu Guoguang. Sydney: Allen and Unwin, 1992.

Yamazawa, Ippei. "On Pacific Economic Integration". *Economic Journal* 102, no. 415 (1992): 1519-29.

Whalley, John. "Regional Trade Arrangements in North America: CUSTA and NAFTA". Paper presented at the World BankCPER Conference on New Dimensions in Regional Integration, Washington, 2-3 April 1992.

Winters, Alan. "The European Community: A Case of Successful Integration?" World BankCPER Conference on New Dimensions in Regional Integration, Washington, 2-3 April 1992.

World Bank. *World Development Report.* Washington, D.C., 1992.

## ABOUT THE AUTHOR

ROSS GARNAUT is Professor and Head of the Department of Economics in the Australian National University's Research School of Pacific Studies. He works on international economics and development in the Asia-Pacific region. Other books in related fields include *Australia and the Northeast Asian Ascendancy*; *ASEAN in a Changing Pacific and World Economy*; (with Kym Anderson) *Australian Protectionism: Extent, Causes and Effects*; (with Liu Guoguang) *Economic Reform and Internationalisation: China in the Pacific Region*; (with Christopher Findlay) *The Political Economy of Manufacturing Protection: Experiences of ASEAN and Australia*.